CW00341220

The Pocket Book of
ANGELS

The Pocket Book of
ANGELS

The power of a protective presence in your life

ARCTURUS

ARCTURUS

This edition published in 2018 by Arcturus Publishing Limited
26/27 Bickels Yard, 151–153 Bermondsey Street,
London SE1 3HA

ISBN: 978-1-78950-093-6
AD006957UK

Printed in China

Introduction

Bringing wisdom and compassion in equal measure, angels can transform a life either through the example they set or by direct intervention. In the following pages, you will see quotations from leading theologians, philosophers and writers, as well as remarkable stories of angelic intervention in the modern world.

Around our pillows golden ladders rise,
And up and down the skies,
With winged sandals shod,
The angels come, and go, the
messengers of God!

Richard Henry Stoddard

An Angel, then, is an intelligent essence, in perpetual motion, with free will, incorporeal, ministering to God, having obtained by grace an immortal nature; and the Creator alone knew the form and limitation of its nature.

St. John

An angel is a spiritual creature created by God without a body for the service of Christendom and the church.

Martin Luther

> *Every visible thing in this world is put in the charge of an angel.*
>
> St. Augustine

From the east to the west sped those angels of the Dawn, from sea to sea, from mountain-top to mountain-top, scattering light from breast and wing.

H. Rider Haggard

Their wings betoken their coming to mankind as messengers, but their haloes symbolize that they come from heaven, which is their home.

Mortimer J. Adler

All arrangements that are carried out between heaven and earth are carried out through angels.

Mirza Ghulam Ahmad

Angels, from the realms of
    glory,
Wing your flight o'er all the
    earth;
Ye who sang creation's story,
Now proclaim Messiah's birth.

James Montgomery

What know we of
the Blest above
But that they sing,
and that they love?

William Wordsworth

The angels in the celestial kingdom have vastly more knowledge and wisdom than the angels in the spiritual kingdom. The celestial angels do not think and speak from faith, like the spiritual angels, but from an internal perception that a thing is so.

Emanuel Swedenborg

Those clouds are angels' robes. —That fiery west
Is paved with smiling faces.

Charles Kingsley

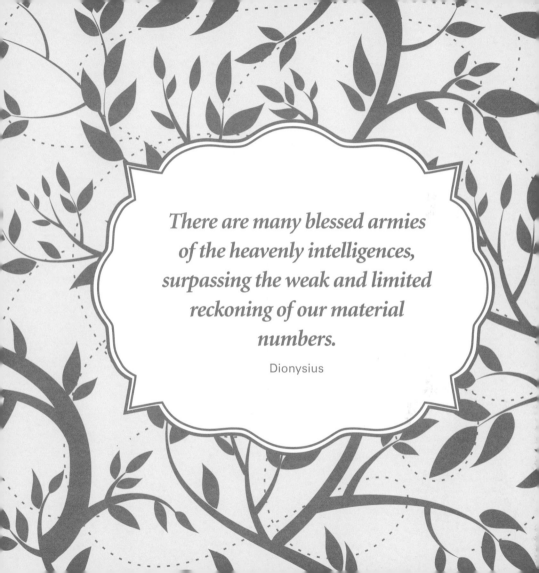

There are many blessed armies of the heavenly intelligences, surpassing the weak and limited reckoning of our material numbers.

Dionysius

When it is said that all things, even the angels, would lapse into nothing unless preserved by God, it is not to be gathered therefrom that there is any principle of corruption in the angels; but that the nature of the angels is dependent upon God as its cause.

St. Thomas Aquinas

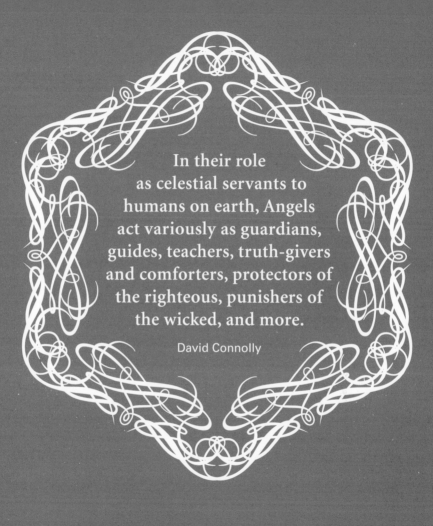

In their role
as celestial servants to
humans on earth, Angels
act variously as guardians,
guides, teachers, truth-givers
and comforters, protectors of
the righteous, punishers of
the wicked, and more.

David Connolly

A demon holds a book in which are written the sins of a particular man; an Angel drops on it, from a phial, a tear which the sinner had shed in doing a good action, and his sins are washed out.

Alberic the Monk

Angels mean messengers and ministers. Their function is to execute the plan of Divine providence, even in earthly things.

St. Thomas Aquinas

The entire hierarchy of Angels can best be described as an endlessly vast sphere of beings who surround an unknowable center point which is called God.

Malcolm Godwin

In such green palaces the
   first kings reign'd,
Slept in their shades, and
   angels entertain'd;
With such old counsellors
   they did advise.
And by frequenting sacred
   groves grew wise.

Edmund Waller

The function of the wing is to take what
is heavy and raise it up into the region
above, where the gods dwell; of all things
connected with the body, it has the
greatest affinity with the divine.

Plato

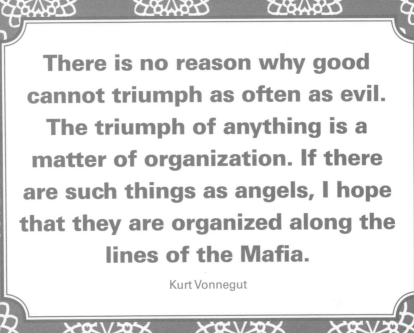

There is no reason why good cannot triumph as often as evil. The triumph of anything is a matter of organization. If there are such things as angels, I hope that they are organized along the lines of the Mafia.

Kurt Vonnegut

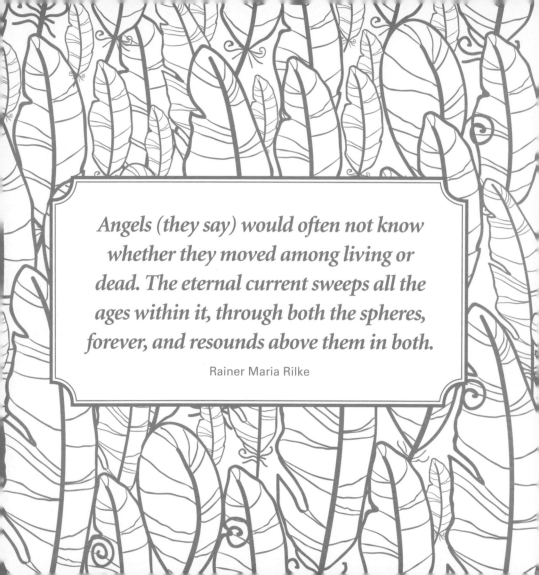

Angels (they say) would often not know whether they moved among living or dead. The eternal current sweeps all the ages within it, through both the spheres, forever, and resounds above them in both.

Rainer Maria Rilke

And this is all that is known, and more than all – yet nothing to what the angels know – of the life of a servant of God, who sinned and repented, and did penance and washed out his sins, and became a saint, and reigns with Christ in heaven.

Cardinal Newman

Angels are not merely forms of extraterrestrial intelligence. They are forms of extra-cosmic intelligence.

Mortimer J. Adler

'HER VOICE WAS SO LOVELY…'

Many years ago, my husband was seriously ill. He had been hospitalized many times and we knew that his time was short. I stayed with him day and night in his hospital room.

One night, he was feeling very low and said he felt so alone. I tried to convince him that he was not alone, that God knew where he was and loved him. About three o'clock in the morning, the door to his room opened and in walked what I thought was a nurse. She went to his bedside and called him by his nickname, a name only his close family and friends knew. She told him that God was there with him and loved him dearly. She asked what his favourite song was. He told her 'Amazing Grace'. There, in the early morning hours, she began to sing. Her voice was so lovely it seemed to fill the room. You could feel the love radiating in the whole room as she sang.

She finished the song, turned and walked quietly out of the room. I wanted to thank her for her kindness and followed her out into the hall. But the hallway was empty and there was no one in sight. I waited for a few minutes, as I thought she had gone into another room. Finally I went to the nurses' station and asked to speak to the nurse who had come into our room. The nurse on duty said that she was the only one assigned to those rooms. Then I knew that God had sent one of his angels to comfort my husband and myself in our time of need.

At the round earth's imagined corners, blow
Your trumpets, angels, and arise, arise
From death, you numberless infinities
Of souls, and to your scattered bodies go.

John Donne

*I saw the angels heave up
Sir Lancelot unto heaven,
and the gates of heaven
opened against him.*

Sir Thomas Malory

It must be known that all spirits and angels without exception were once men, for the human race is the seminary of heaven; and that spirits are altogether such as to their affections and inclinations as they had been when they lived as men in the world, for every one's life follows him.

Emanuel Swedenborg

'YOU ARE GOING TO BE OK'

When I was about 19, I started using drugs and really beginning to abuse myself physically and mentally. As time went on, my older sister became concerned and asked me to hang out with her more often, but I always made excuses to avoid her. When I finally agreed to spend the evening with her, she had arranged a blind date for me. The day before I was supposed to meet her, I went to a party that lasted until the following day.

I remember a few things about that night as I lay in my bed: the pain my body was feeling, my sister calling me

 to tell me my blind date was waiting, and an image at the foot of my bed as I begged for the pain to go away. It was one of those moments when you cannot tell if it is a dream or if it is real. I was restless. I fell asleep, then

woke up to see two people at the foot of my bed. There was a girl on my left side and a boy on my right. They would not look at my face, but just stood there with their heads tilted and said, 'Don't worry, you are going to be OK.'

I woke up the next day to realize a lot about myself and to know those changes could not happen in a day. I am 30 now and drug free. There are many gaps to fill in this story, but I would just like to mention that there are angels out there – whether they be in your dreams or at the foot of your bed.

One more thing: that blind date I was supposed to meet that night? He is the man I am married to now. This is a man who has also brought faith back into my life.

God does not deal directly with man: it is by means of spirits that all the intercourse and communication of gods with men, both in waking life and in sleep, is carried on.

Socrates

In the strictest definition, an angel is a superior being living in the spirit world – standing between humans and God.

John Ronner

It is not plainly said whether or when the angels were created; but if mention is made, it is implicit under the name of 'heaven,' when it is said, 'In the beginning God created the heavens and the earth.'

St. Augustine

Bless the Lord, all you angels,
mighty in strength and
attentive, obedient to every
command.

Psalm 103.20

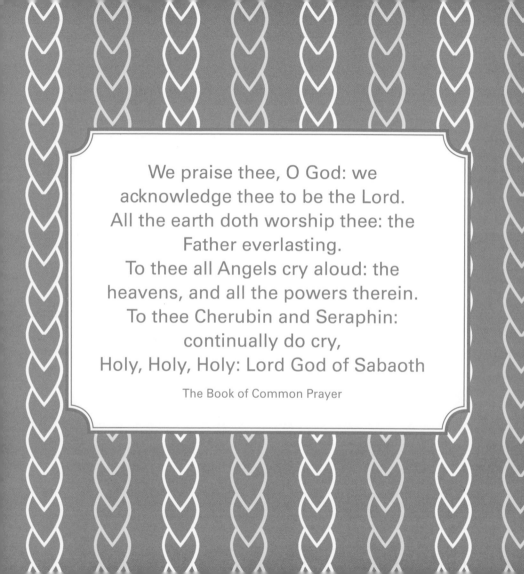

We praise thee, O God: we acknowledge thee to be the Lord.
All the earth doth worship thee: the Father everlasting.
To thee all Angels cry aloud: the heavens, and all the powers therein.
To thee Cherubin and Seraphin: continually do cry,
Holy, Holy, Holy: Lord God of Sabaoth

The Book of Common Prayer

May Michael be at my right hand and
Gabriel at my left, before me Uriel and
Raphael behind, and above my head
the divine presence of God.

Jewish prayer

To worship at the feet of the angels, when
all men worship only fame and riches, is
not easy. But the most difficult of all is to
think the thoughts of the angels, to speak
the words of the angels, and to do as the
angels do.

Gospel of the Essenes

For thou hast made him a little lower than the angels, and hast crowned him with glory and honour.

Psalm 8:5

 33

'THEY HAD THIS GLOW ABOUT THEM...'

A couple of years ago, my parents and I had been shopping. We decided to take the back roads and go the long way home to skip the highways. We heard a big pop and dad got out of the car and saw we had a flat. We were in the middle of nowhere, with no one to be seen, miles from the nearest home or stores. We had no extra tire and it was pitch black outside.

After a few minutes, two young men stopped their car and asked if we needed help. They were very kind and

gentle; almost non-human. They had this glow about them. They had an extra tire the exact size we needed and they fixed our flat like they had done it a million times before. We told them thank you, and asked if there was anything we could do for them. They told us that we all get in trouble sometimes and there was no need to thank them. They gave my dad a pat on the back and gave me and mom a hug and said, 'God bless you, God is with you', then disappeared into thin air. We looked everywhere for them. I don't know what happened that night, but I believe those men were angels and they were watching over us. All I can say is it was a miracle.

FELLOW PASSENGER

I live in Toronto, Canada. I had taken the streetcar down town because I was going for a job interview. As I approached my destination, it began to snow so heavily I couldn't see. Just before getting to my stop, I got up and went to the door. I tried to look for traffic, but couldn't see anything. Beside me on the stairs was a man who I assumed would be getting off at the same stop.

The doors opened at my stop and I was about to get

off when I noticed that the man made no move. I was distracted by this. At that moment, a tractor trailer whizzed by the streetcar. I thought, 'Oh my gosh – I could have been killed!'

I turned to thank the man, but he had vanished. I asked others on the bus if they had seen the man, but they said there was nobody there. I am convinced that God sent an angel. If he had not been there, I would have stepped off and been killed instantly.

> *For He shall give his angels charge over thee,*
> *to keep thee in all thy ways.*
>
> Psalm 91:11

Now long ago I sat and listened to the angels at this hour, and marvelled how they cried out; their cry was like the noise of a mighty wheel, and they cried out like the waves of the sea with the voice of praise to God.

The Testament of Adam

**Every blade of grass has an
angel that bends over it and
whispers, 'grow! grow!'**

The Talmud

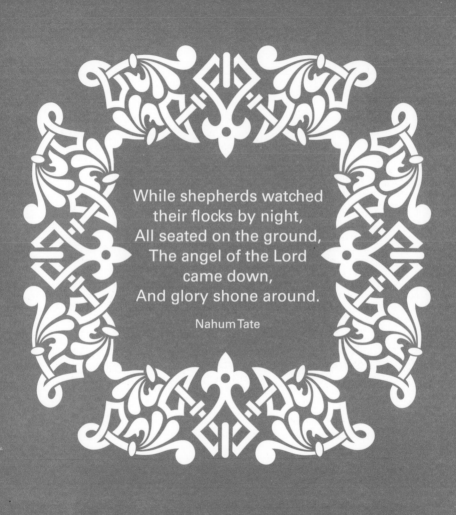

While shepherds watched
their flocks by night,
All seated on the ground,
The angel of the Lord
came down,
And glory shone around.

Nahum Tate

Those who have said, 'Our
Lord is God', then have gone
straight, upon them the
angels descend, saying, 'Fear
not, neither sorrow; rejoice
in Paradise that you were
promised. We are your
friends in the present life
and in the world to come;
therein you shall have all
that your souls desire…'

The Koran

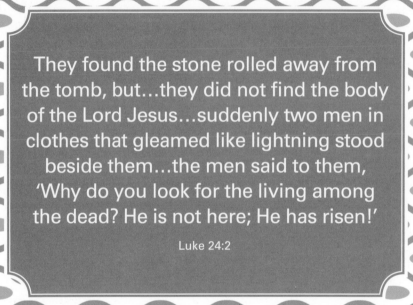

They found the stone rolled away from the tomb, but…they did not find the body of the Lord Jesus…suddenly two men in clothes that gleamed like lightning stood beside them…the men said to them, 'Why do you look for the living among the dead? He is not here; He has risen!'

Luke 24:2

Behold, I send an Angel before thee, to keep thee in the way, and to bring thee into the place which I have prepared.

Exodus 23:20

'SOMEONE PICKED UP THE PHONE…'

My mother is 82 and has a rare form of cancer and several other illnesses. She is the most loving, generous woman I know, but has had such an unhappy life, mentally and physically. She stays with me five days a week and goes to her apartment at weekends.

Last Saturday she mentioned she was feeling dizzy and a bit unwell. This happens often, so I told her to rest and said I would phone her later.

I was walking my dog at a park near her apartment when I called her on my cell phone. Her phone rang at least 25 times. I knew she was there and became worried when she didn't answer. I called again and, after about 13 rings, someone picked up the phone. Very faintly in the background I could hear her calling my name. I asked if she was hurt. I could hear her saying that she had fallen and was on the kitchen floor. I told her I would be right there. But how had she answered the phone?

When I got to her apartment I found my mom on the floor and both phones still on the hook. She could not have moved to answer them! She lives alone and no one else was there. Whoever picked up the phone saved my mom's life. I thank God and my mom's guardian angels for allowing my call to get through to her. I believe in miracles, but I'm still numb from this experience.

The cherubim shall spread out their wings above, overshadowing the mercy seat with their wings, their faces one to another; toward the mercy seat shall the faces of the cherubim be.

Exodus 25:20

O come, all ye faithful,
Joyful and triumphant,
O come ye, O come ye to Bethlehem;
Come and behold him,
Born the King of angels.

A carol from Murray's Hymnal

Neither can they die any more: for they are equal unto the angels.

Luke 20:36

A CALM PRESENCE

Twelve years ago, I had a small apartment and lived alone. One night I had a sudden feeling of dread as I was lying in bed. A dark figure approached and lay down on top of me. I could not breathe or move. I was horrified. This thing looked three-dimensional, but was made of shadow. It was terrifying. I prayed very hard for it to go away.

Suddenly, something came and sat on my bed. I could not see a figure, but could see the indentation of where it was sitting and

actually felt the bed move. A feeling of calm and serenity came over me. All I felt was love, and that everything was going to be OK.
I fell into a deep sleep and woke up the next morning still feeling like there was a calm presence in the room.

It took me almost a year to tell my boyfriend, now my husband, about the incident. I thought he would think I was crazy. But I think it was an angel sent by God to protect me from this evil entity.

O sovereign angel,
Wide winged stranger
above a forgetful earth,
Care for me, care for me,
Keep me unaware of danger

Edna St. Vincent Millay

And lo, the angel of the Lord came upon them, and the glory of the Lord shone round about them, and they were sore afraid. And the angel said unto them, 'Fear not, for behold, I bring you good tidings of great joy, which shall be to all people. For unto you is born this day in the City of David a Saviour, who is Christ the Lord.'

Luke 2:9

We cannot pass our
guardian angel's bounds,
Resigned or sullen, he will hear our sighs.

John Keble

Who are these angels? They are his guardians
from the harmful spirits; as it is said,
'A thousand shall fall at your side and ten thousand at your right hand.'

The Midrash

Sleep, my child, and peace attend thee
All through the night.
Guardian angels God will send thee,
All through the night.

Sir Harold Boulton

We're all kissed by angels, but some of us never think to pucker.

Amethyst Snow-Rivers

The servants of Christ are protected by invisible, rather than visible, beings. But if these guard you, they do so because they have been summoned by your prayer.

St. Ambrose

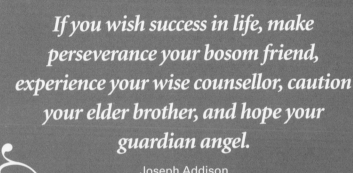

If you wish success in life, make perseverance your bosom friend, experience your wise counsellor, caution your elder brother, and hope your guardian angel.

Joseph Addison

**For God commands the angels
to guard you in all your ways.**

Psalms 91:11

Angels are inseparable friends, who bring strength and consolation to those who include them in their lives. In truth, angels are our best friends.

Janice T. Connell

If we truly love our Guardian Angel, we cannot fail to have boundless confidence in his powerful intercession with God and firm faith in his willingness to help us.

St. Bernard of Clairveaux

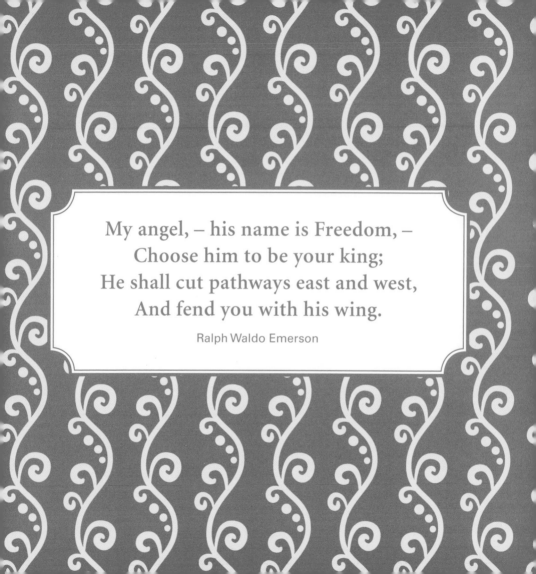

My angel, – his name is Freedom, –
Choose him to be your king;
He shall cut pathways east and west,
And fend you with his wing.

Ralph Waldo Emerson

Angels and ministers of grace defend us.

William Shakespeare

God assures us that his angels are always nearby, ready to help. This is what matters.

Timothy Jones

The angel of the Lord encampeth round about them that fear Him, and delivereth them.

Psalm 34:7

We not only live among men, but there are airy hosts, blessed spectators, sympathetic lookers-on, that see and know and appreciate our thoughts and feelings and acts.

Henry Ward Beecher

Let your holy Angel have charge concerning us, that the wicked one have no power over us.

Martin Luther

'SOMEONE WAS PUSHING ME OUT OF BED...'

My wife's nephew, Roger, came to stay with us for the night. He was only around three or four at the time. Roger really liked to come visit and play with our younger son, who was a few years older than him.

In the middle of the night, I felt someone trying to push me out of bed. I heard a voice saying, 'Look for Roger, look for Roger', so I jumped out of bed and went to my son's room. Roger was nowhere to be seen. I woke my wife and she went and looked in our son's room again.

I went down to the living room to find the front door wide open. As I walked through it, I looked to my left and saw Roger walking down the sidewalk, about to turn the corner. I yelled out to my wife, who ran after him and brought him home. I really don't know why he walked out of the apartment that day – I guess he was sleep-walking.

This experience has made me a more spiritual person. I truly believe a guardian angel was sent to look after Roger that night.

ANGELIC HANDS

When I was about nine years old my mother took me down to a creek near our house so I could cool off and have fun on a very hot summer's day. I didn't know how to swim, but I enjoyed playing in the water.

I was standing on a big rock when my feet slipped and I fell in the water and went under. Every time I came up I tried to yell for help but couldn't get the word out before I went under again. I know I went under the water three times, but it could have been four.

All of a sudden I felt hands under my arms. It was a physical feeling as though a person was helping me. When I had my feet solidly back on the rock, the hands disappeared. I turned round to say 'thank you', but there was no one there. The closest people were sitting on the bank on the other side of the creek, about two hundred feet away. And I turned round just a few seconds after the hands had gone.

There is no doubt in my mind that an angel saved me that day from drowning.

How wonderful it must be, to speak the language of Angels, with no words for hate and a million words for love!

Eileen Elias Freeman

Death makes angels of us all and gives us wings where we had shoulders smooth as ravens' claws.

Jim Morrison

Angels help you laugh at life, even when you don't think it's funny.

Karen Goldman

We shall find peace. We shall hear the angels, we shall see the sky sparkling with diamonds.

Anton Chekhov

The guardian angels of life fly so high as to be beyond our sight, but they are always looking down upon us.

Jean Paul Richter

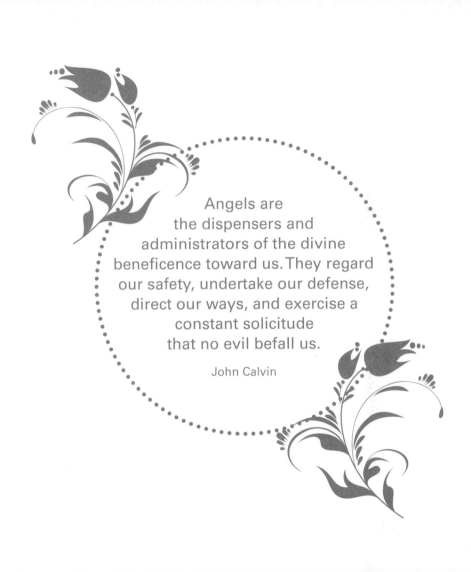

Angels are
the dispensers and
administrators of the divine
beneficence toward us. They regard
our safety, undertake our defense,
direct our ways, and exercise a
constant solicitude
that no evil befall us.

John Calvin

The dignity of human souls is great, for each has an angel appointed to guard it.

St. Jerome

The wings of angels are often found on the backs of the least likely people.

Eric Honeycutt

Have you ever considered that, just perhaps, the reason you have gotten as far as you have is because of the invisible work of anonymous Angels? Good strangers in the night?

Gary Kinnaman

> **If you find it impossible to pray, charge your Good Angel to pray in your stead.**
>
> St. John Vianney

Becoming aware of our angels' hidden presence in our lives is not difficult or arduous, but it is subtle and requires great patience.

Eileen Elias Freeman

All God's angels
come to us
disguised.

James Russell Lowe

Angels are messengers,
but sometimes we
misunderstand their
language.

Linda Solegato

Since God often
sends us inspirations
by means of
Angels, we should
frequently return our
aspirations to God by
means of the same
messengers.

St. Francis de Sales

Perhaps children's innocence, wherever it comes from, contributes to the fact that they seem to see angels more often.

John Ronner

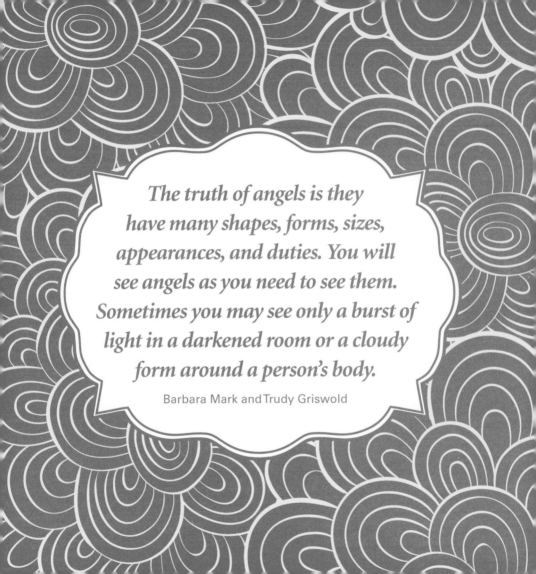

The truth of angels is they have many shapes, forms, sizes, appearances, and duties. You will see angels as you need to see them. Sometimes you may see only a burst of light in a darkened room or a cloudy form around a person's body.

Barbara Mark and Trudy Griswold

Though angels are both the messengers and the message of God, that makes them no easier to receive. For one thing, we almost never recognize them, even when they knock at our door.

F. Forrester Church

As the spirit blows where it will, so do angels ride the winds of spontaneity.

Maria Parisen

A TRAVELLING COMPANION

One of the most famous people to believe in angels is the current pontiff, Pope Francis. He told the crowds who gathered to celebrate the Feast of Holy Guardian Angels in 2014 that he considered his own guardian angel to be his 'travelling companion'.

He said: 'Often times, we have the feeling, "I shouldn't do this…this is not right…be careful". This is the voice of our guardian angel. Do not rebel: follow his advice. No one walks alone and none of us can think that he is alone, because this companion is always with us. It is dangerous to chase away our travelling companion, because no man, no woman can advise themselves.

I can give advice to another, but I cannot give advice to myself. The Holy Spirit [is] the angel who advises me. This is why we need him.'

Pope Francis suggested we should all ask ourselves the question: 'How is my relationship with my guardian angel? Do I listen to him? Do I wish him good morning? Do I say: "Protect me during sleep"? Do I speak with him? Do I ask his advice? He is at my side. We can respond to this question today, each and everyone of us: "How is my relationship with this angel who the Lord has sent to protect and accompany me along the way, and who always sees the face of the Father who is in the heavens?"'

THE LOST MONEY ORDER

While relaxing in my mother in-law's back yard, I remembered I had left the money order for that month's rent in the back pocket of the jeans I had been wearing the previous day.

Upon arriving home, I immediately went upstairs to retrieve the order so I could mail it before it was late. I found my jeans and looked in all the pockets – no money order. I couldn't find it anywhere! My husband and I searched the entire house – all in vain.

I was devastated. At this time my husband was disabled, unable to work. I was the only one working. All I could think was that I had three beautiful young children who were going to be homeless if I didn't find that money order.

I got down on my knees at the side of our bed and prayed. I spoke to God and pleaded, 'Lord you know that I am trying…I cannot come up with this rent again. Please, Lord, help me find this money order.' On finishing my prayer, I opened my eyes. Then I saw the most amazing thing I have ever experienced in my entire life. On the bed, right in front of my eyes lay a white piece of paper. I reached for the paper, turned it over, and indeed it was the lost money order.

I am not crazy – I know this money order was not there before I knelt to pray. My guardian angel was there for me. I have never doubted the presence of higher beings since then. And never will!

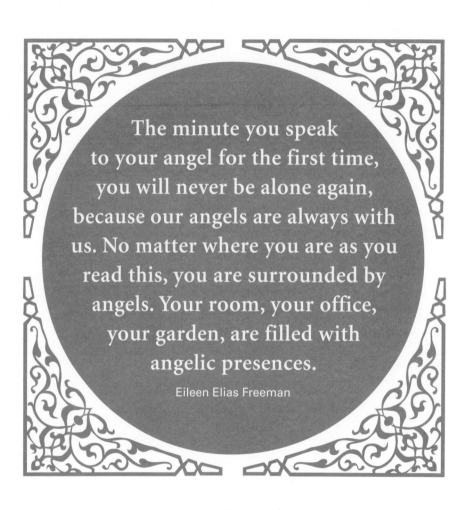

The minute you speak
to your angel for the first time,
you will never be alone again,
because our angels are always with
us. No matter where you are as you
read this, you are surrounded by
angels. Your room, your office,
your garden, are filled with
angelic presences.

Eileen Elias Freeman

I throw myself down in my chamber, and I call in, and invite God, and his Angels thither, and when they are there, I neglect God and his Angels, for the noise of a fly, for the rattling of a coach, for the whining of a door.

John Donne

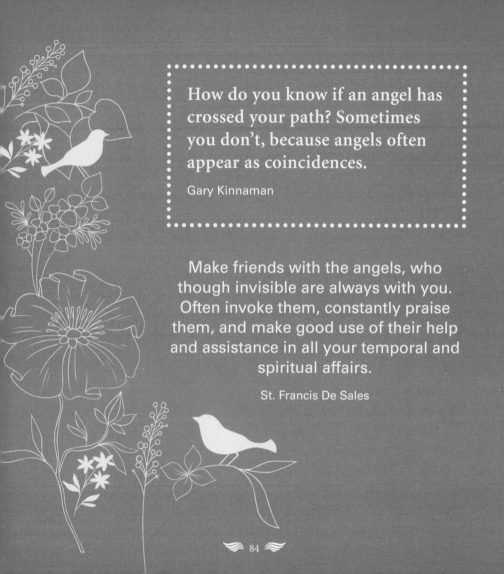

How do you know if an angel has crossed your path? Sometimes you don't, because angels often appear as coincidences.

Gary Kinnaman

Make friends with the angels, who though invisible are always with you. Often invoke them, constantly praise them, and make good use of their help and assistance in all your temporal and spiritual affairs.

St. Francis De Sales

Monsters will always exist. There's one inside each of us. But an angel lives there, too. There is no more important agenda than figuring out how to slay one and nurture the other.

Jacqueline Novogratz

As one truly learns to speak the language of the angels, he finds he can also walk and talk with God, and he can hold his place in the realms of light. He casts out all fear and darkness from his soul.

Annalee Skarin

I have seen a thousand times that Angels are human form, or men, for I have conversed with them as man to man, sometimes with one alone, sometimes with many in company.

Emanuel Swedenborg

Whatever you put your attention on in this life will increase in your life. As you put your attention on angels, they will begin increasingly to make their presence known to you.

Denise Linn

MOTHER'S DAY ANGEL

In 2007 my husband and I lost our only son. It was a devastating time. He was only a month old when he passed. A week later, on Mother's Day, my parents were out of town and my husband was at work, also in another town. I went to the cemetery by myself. My son's headstone was not there yet. I was sitting by a pile of dirt, hunched over crying uncontrollably, when I felt someone wrap their arms around me and hug me.

I turned to find an older woman behind me. I said, 'This is my first Mother's Day and all I have is a pile of dirt!'

The woman told me things would be OK and that I'd make it through and would have another child. She walked away and came back with a rose. She said it was for my son, but she added she thought I needed it more. Then she left. I had not told her that I had a son.

I've been to the cemetery many times since then, but haven't seen her again. I don't know if she was an angel or not, but she was an angel to me! My husband and I now have a wonderful two-and-a-half-year-old child.

It is in rugged crises, in unweariable endurance, and in aims which put sympathy out of the question, that the angel is shown.

Ralph Waldo Emerson

Even the highest angels
seek out and learn
mysteries of grace.

St. Thomas Aquinas

I think it's obvious that
there is demon and angel
in all. And they are all
around us, too. It is like
beauty being in the eye of
the beholder.

Brychan Llyr

'YOU ARE NOT ALONE...'

I went through a life-shattering divorce soon after the birth of my son. I was living in Atlanta, Georgia, at the time, and my family was living in Chicago. My husband had left several weeks earlier and I was getting ready to move out. I had loaded my things onto a removal truck and was spending the last few days with my infant son at a girlfriend's house. I was selling our house and moving back to Chicago. It was a very dark time.

My friend dropped us at the airport and we said goodbye. I was leaving so much behind: my marriage, my friends, my home and my job. I felt so alone as she drove away.

I put my son in his stroller and began walking down the sidewalk to the terminal. As I was walking along, I felt two firm taps on my shoulder. I turned round quickly only to find that no one was there. No one was even near me! At that very second I heard the words, 'You are not alone.' These words were not audible – they came as a loud inner voice, but it was not my own 'thinking voice'. The taps were as real as anything, though – so firm that they were just shy of uncomfortable.

A feeling of love swept over me. I smiled and was reassured, and boarded the plane feeling much lighter. I have not felt alone in that way since then.

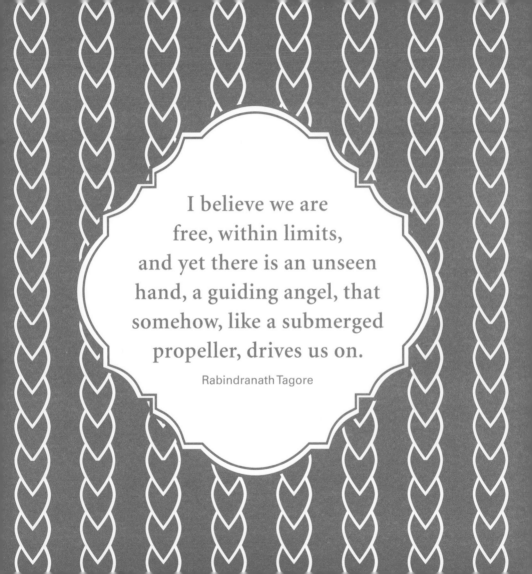

I believe we are
free, within limits,
and yet there is an unseen
hand, a guiding angel, that
somehow, like a submerged
propeller, drives us on.

Rabindranath Tagore

Angels deliver Fate to our doorstep –
and anywhere else it is needed.

Jessi Lane Adams

The Present, the Present
is all thou hast
For thy sure possessing;
Like the patriarch's angel
hold it fast
Till it gives its blessing.

John Greenleaf Whittier

It is not because angels are holier than men or devils that makes them angels, but because they do not expect holiness from one another, but from God only.

William Blake

Ambition first sprung from your blest abodes;

The glorious fault of angels and of gods.

Alexander Pope

Give of yourself as the Angels do, and wonderful things will come to you.

Ramadan

A BRIGHT LIGHT

My parents both died three years ago, just four months apart. My mother was diagnosed with cancer the day after my dad was buried. It was a shock and she was devastated; not only had she lost her husband of 57 years, she would not live to see my children grow up. She was not ready to die. The months passed, and I mourned terribly for both of them. I prayed and prayed for a sign that they were OK, and that they knew I could be OK.

The night before last, I was asleep in my bed. My five-year-old son had

climbed in bed with us. We have
an old lamp by the bed that won't
turn on easily. In the middle of the
night I was awakened suddenly by a
bright light. When I sat up I saw that
the old lamp was on, and shining
so bright it was blinding. I reached
over and shut it off so as not to wake my son. I lay
back down puzzled, and looked at my alarm clock – it
was 3:38 a.m. Then I realized the date was January 21.
The exact date and time of my mother's death, three
years ago.

I suddenly felt like my chest was full and my heart
was going to burst right out. I realized my mother had
come to let me know she was OK, and that I should be
too. I will never ever forget that feeling, or forget the
brightness of that light.

That's all an angel
is, an idea of God.

Meister Eckhart

Man is made a little lower than the angels, and yet with the ability of choice, and thus may turn those conditions or positions or associations into hell or heaven, according to the use of same.

Edgar Cayce

IN A BETTER PLACE

My grandfather had been fighting stomach cancer for years, but on March 21, 2006, the battle ended for him. Before he died, my mom had been to visit him. She told him she would be fine after his death if he could give her a sign telling her that he was OK.

About two weeks later, my mom was at work and the song 'Angel' by Sarah McLachlan came on the radio. A ray of sunshine fell across my mom's face and she turned to her co-worker and told her she thought her dad

had just passed away. Five minutes later, she got a call from her sister saying that their dad had died.

We said our sad goodbyes, but we knew he wasn't in pain any more and that he was in a better place. On the one-year anniversary of his death, my mom was at work and the same song, 'Angel', came on the radio. My mom noticed that it was at the exact time of day her dad had died. She got goose bumps and looked up and said, 'Thank you, dad'.

But we can all be angels to one another. We can choose to obey the still small stirring within, the little whisper that says, 'Go. Ask. Reach out. Be an answer to someone's plea.'

Joan Wester Anderson

Philosophy will clip an angel's wings.

John Keats

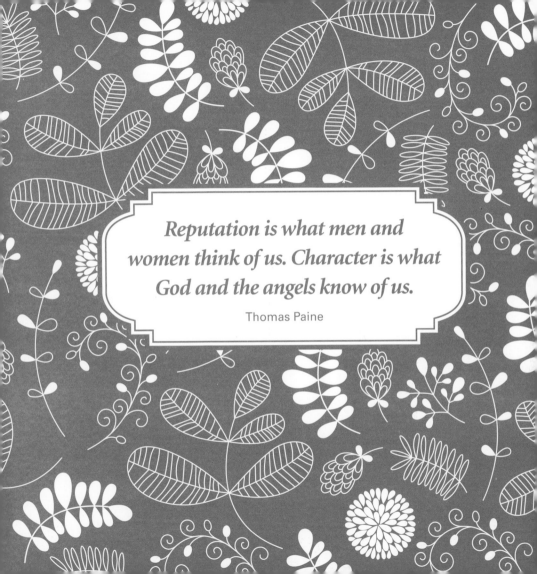

Reputation is what men and women think of us. Character is what God and the angels know of us.

Thomas Paine

We are each of us angels with only one wing. And we can only fly by embracing each other.

Luciano de Crescenzo

Think, in mounting higher,
The angels would press on us, and aspire
To drop some golden orb of perfect song
Into our deep, dear silence.

Elizabeth Barrett Browning

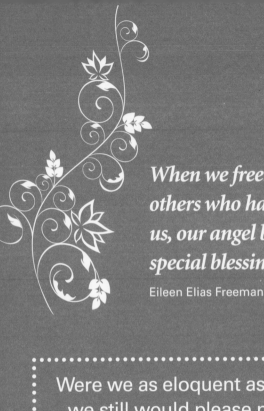

When we freely forgive others who have hurt us, our angel brings us a special blessing of love.

Eileen Elias Freeman

Were we as eloquent as angels we still would please people much more by listening rather than talking.

Charles Caleb Colton

We trust in plumed procession,
For such the angels go —

Rank after Rank, with even feet
And uniforms of Snow.

Emily Dickinson

If instead of a gem, or even a flower, we should cast the gift of a loving thought into the heart of a friend, that would be giving as the angels give.

George MacDonald

Have you ever seen a flower down
Sometimes angels skip around
And in their blissful state of glee
Bump into a daisy or sweet pea?

Jessi Lane Adams

DEEP WATER

Our pastor had taken his family to the coast for a well-deserved holiday. The adults were sitting on the beach and the kids were playing in the waves. Their eldest girl (a teenager) went in deeper than the rest and was swimming just behind the breakers. The tide grabbed her and within minutes she was dragged out into very deep water.

People saw what was happening and started shouting for the lifeguards. Thirty-five minutes later, the girl was dragged out onto the beach. She had a remarkable story to tell. According to her, as the current got hold of her, she could feel herself being dragged deeper and could see the people on the beach getting smaller. As she tried to fight

the tide and swim back to shore, a man appeared next to her. He said that all she was doing was tiring herself out. He told her to calm down and stop trying to fight the current. He was a young man with long blond hair, but he had a full white beard.

Once she had calmed down, the young man told her he couldn't help her, but he would stay with her till the lifeguards arrived. After she had been rescued and was safely on dry land, she asked for the blond man in order to thank him. But the lifeguards said she had been the only person in the sea when they found her.

If an angel were
ever to tell us
anything of his
philosophy, I believe
many propositions would
sound like two times
two equals three.

Georg C. Lichtenberg

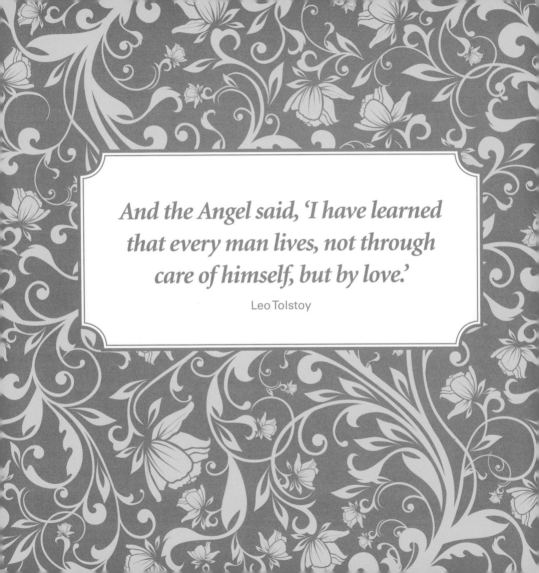

And the Angel said, 'I have learned that every man lives, not through care of himself, but by love.'

Leo Tolstoy

In the case of those who are making progress from good to better, the good angel touches the soul gently, lightly, sweetly, as a drop of water enters a sponge.

St. Ignatius of Loyola

The angels see you as dazzling young diamonds which are being polished to perfection.

Elsa Joy Bailey

You'll meet more angels on a winding path than on a straight one.

Daisey Verlaef

YELLOW BUTTERFLY

When my boyfriend and I were planning our wedding, my grandmother became ill. On her deathbed, she asked my boyfriend to promise to bring God into my life. He said he would, and he has fulfilled that promise.

On the day of our wedding, a yellow butterfly was seen during the whole ceremony (which was held in my parents' back yard). During important parts of the ceremony, the butterfly landed on my butt! We thought it was pretty funny – nothing could stop it going right back! After the wedding, we greeted our guests and kept seeing that butterfly around us. We all made jokes about it. Then, while the photographer was taking pictures, the butterfly landed on my husband's shoulder. We have a picture of him smiling with a bright yellow butterfly beautifully positioned on his shoulder. We never thought too much of it.

We have been married almost seven years now. It seems that every time I cry out for God to help me through a crisis, I look up and see a bright, beautiful, yellow butterfly. I have seen it more than 100 times during my marriage. I cannot remember ever seeing one at all until my wedding day.

All I know is that I love that yellow butterfly. To me, it means, 'Everything is going to be all right.'

I will not wish thee riches, nor the
glow of greatness,
But that wherever thou go some weary
heart shall gladden at thy smile,
Or shadowed life know sunshine
for a while.
And so thy path shall be a track of light,
Like angels' footsteps passing through
the night.

Words on an English church wall

It is not known precisely where the angels dwell – whether in the air, the void, or the planets. It has not been God's pleasure that we should be informed of their abode.

Voltaire

If I got rid of my demons, I'd lose my angels.

Tennessee Williams

The more materialistic science
becomes, the more angels shall
I paint. Their wings are my protest in
favour of the immortality of the soul.

Edward Burne-Jones

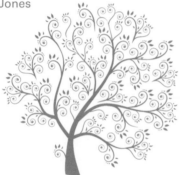

**Outside the open window
The morning air is all
awash with angels.**

Richard Wilbur

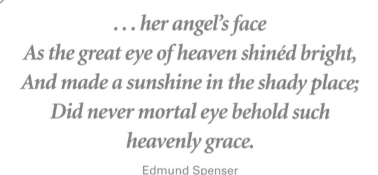

... her angel's face
As the great eye of heaven shinéd bright,
And made a sunshine in the shady place;
Did never mortal eye behold such
heavenly grace.

Edmund Spenser

Oh woman! lovely woman! Nature made thee
To temper man: we had been brutes
without you;
Angels are painted fair, to look like you;
There's in you all that we believe of heaven,
Amazing brightness, purity, and truth,
Eternal joy, and everlasting love.

Thomas Otway

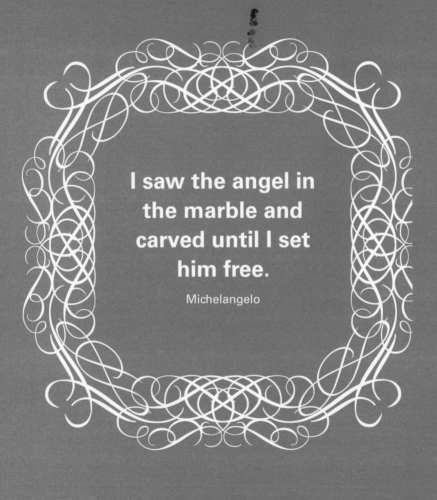

I saw the angel in the marble and carved until I set him free.

Michelangelo

Kind words are the
music of the world. They have
a power which seems to be beyond
natural causes, as if they were some
angel's song, which had lost its way
and come on Earth, and sang on
undyingly, smiting the hearts of men
with sweetest wounds, and putting
for the while an angel's
nature into us.

Frederick William Faber

Cease every joy, to glimmer on my mind,
But leave, oh leave the light of Hope behind!
What though my winged hours of bliss have been,
Like angel visits, few and far between.

Thomas Campbell

The angels are calling us up. We are meant to fly and with our spirits we can. We are meant to ascend, to transmute the negative mass of the world's corrupted thought forms. No one asked us to stay so long, away from heaven, away from joy.

Marianne Williamson